Quick Start

M000021195

The Essential
BLOOD SUGAR
DIET
MEALS FOR ONE

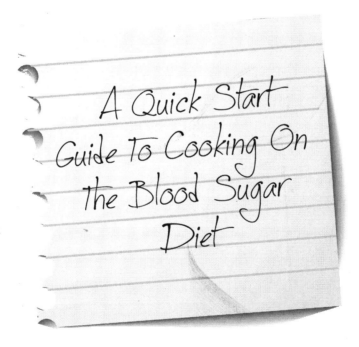

A Quick Start
Guide To Cooking On
the Blood Sugar
Diet

**Over 80 Easy And Delicious
Calorie Counted Recipes For One
Lose Weight And Rebalance Your Blood Sugar**

First published in 2016 by Erin Rose Publishing

Text and illustration copyright © 2016 Erin Rose Publishing

Design: Julie Anson

ISBN: 978-1-911492-01-6

A CIP record for this book is available from the British Library.

DISCLAIMER: This book is for informational purposes only and not intended as a substitute for the medical advice, diagnosis or treatment of a physician or qualified healthcare provider. The reader should consult a physician before undertaking a new health care regime and in all matters relating to his/her health, and particularly with respect to any symptoms that may require diagnosis or medical attention.

While every care has been taken in compiling the recipes for this book we cannot accept responsibility for any problems which arise as a result of preparing one of the recipes. The author and publisher disclaim responsibility for any adverse effects that may arise from the use or application of the recipes in this book. Some of the recipes in this book include nuts and eggs. If you have an egg or nut allergy it's important to avoid these. It is recommended that children, pregnant women, the elderly or anyone who has an immune system disorder avoid eating raw eggs.

CONTENTS

Breakfast Recipes

Lunch Recipes

Dinner Recipes

Sweet Treats & Snacks

INTRODUCTION

If you are cooking for one and following the blood sugar diet, whether you live alone or are eating separate meals to the rest of the family, you want something easy and delicious to eat which doesn't take much time or effort. That's why we bring you '**The Essential Blood Sugar Diet, Meals For One**,' making healthy eating at mealtimes simple and delicious! After all, the beauty of cooking for one is you get to eat what you want!

You can tuck into to nutritious blood-sugar friendly meals and snacks especially for solo cooking. Whether you are starting and maintaining a healthy diet or aiming to lose weight, you can choose from plenty of mouth-watering recipes for breakfast, lunch, dinner, snacks and sweet treats which are all calories counted.

Thousands of people world-wide have already benefited from the blood sugar diet and are reaping the benefits of eating to lose weight and balance their blood sugar through sugar-free and low carb foods. Great news for anyone ready to improve their health and lifestyle! You needn't feel hungry, restricted or uninspired because there are so many exciting ways to incorporate a wide range of tasty foods into your diet without wasting ingredients. Are you ready to expand your healthy regime with even more recipes to balance your blood sugar and lose weight? Read on!

Balancing Your Blood Sugar

Whenever we eat, our body's blood sugar level rises in response to the food we've consumed, causing highs and subsequent lows. The effects of excess sugar and carbohydrates and swings in our blood sugar levels can cause changes to our physical and emotional health which can be mild to severe in the long term.

Ideally, severe swings in blood sugar levels should be avoided and therefore the causes; sugar and starchy carbohydrate intake, needs to be managed. This isn't just the case for type 2 diabetes but for anyone with pre-diabetes, obesity, hypoglycaemia and insulin resistance. Some signs and symptoms that you could be experiencing blood sugar problems are:

- Difficulty losing weight despite healthy eating

- Anxiety, foggy thinking, irritability, mood swings and insomnia

- Weakness, fatigue and craving for stimulants such as chocolate, sugar, coffee and cigarettes

- Heart palpitations

- Light headedness, shaking and visual disturbance

- Digestive problems such as bloating and excess wind

- Obesity, pre-diabetes and type 2 diabetes

- High blood pressure, raised cholesterol, heart disease and strokes.

Most people will benefit from reducing their sugar consumption but always consult your doctor about any symptoms you have before making significant dietary changes to check it's right for you.

Kick Start To Great Health

Before you begin, decide what your personal goals are. Is your primary motivation to shed extra weight as well as improving blood sugar levels? If so, you can not only steer clear of the foods on the 'avoid' list AND additionally restrict your calorie intake, to improve and increase healthy weight loss. The key thing you need to do is quit eating sugar, in all its forms and reduce or avoid your intake of refined carbohydrates ie. starchy foods like, pasta, potatoes, bread and cakes.

For some this may be easier said than done because cravings drive you to the kitchen cupboards in search of comfort foods but this is completely manageable. Avoid sugary and starchy foods that cause cravings for stodgy foods and they will subside after a few days, providing you don't give in to them. During that time you could find your mood improves and your vitality increases giving you an encouraging boost to keep going. Once you see your weight begin to decrease to what is healthy and right for you, it will be worth it!

If you choose to limit your calorie intake, aim to consume no more than 1000 calories a day or even less. Calorie restriction will not only speed up weight loss but improve your blood sugar levels faster. Make your blood sugar diet work for you and set a realistic target which you can stick to. Decide what you want to achieve and take action. You can get started straight away.

If your cupboards are crammed with sweet snacks, fizzy drinks and sticky syrups and sauces, you would do well to clear out the temptations unless you have rock solid will power.

If you need proof that you've been consuming more sugar than you thought, especially when you weren't even aware of it, check out the ingredients' labels and count up just how much sugar you've inadvertently been eating. To give you an idea what your sugar consumption looks like, approximately 4g of sugar is approximately one teaspoonful.

Fructose Facts

So we know sugar is harmful but fruit also contains sugar in the form of fructose. One of the main reasons people who eat 'healthily' struggle to lose weight is their fructose consumption because those glasses of orange juice and smoothies can contain vast amounts of sugar and are especially harmful when the fibre has been removed. Fructose is stored as fat in the liver, increases belly mass and plays havoc with blood sugar levels. Yes, fruit is packed with valuable vitamins but keep your intake low, avoid really sweet tropical fruits and eat it with its fibre rather than separating the juice from the fibre.

What Can't I Eat?

Below is a list of the food to AVOID.

CARBOHYDRATES

- Bread
- Cakes
- Cereals
- Cookies
- Crackers
- Millet
- Muesli
- Noodles
- Oats
- Pasta
- Potatoes
- Sweet Potatoes
- Rice

FATS

- Vegetables oils such as corn and canola

- Spreads and margarines which are low fat, contain trans fats or contain sugar

SUGARS

- Avoid products containing sugar, honey, syrup, chocolate bars, sweets and candy.
  Marinades and ready-made sauces like sweet chilli sauces, ketchup, barbecue sauce
  and any dressing containing sugar. Always check the label for added sugar.

- Avoid ripe tropical fruit such as mango and papaya and dried fruit, like apricots,
  sultanas, raisins and figs.

DRINKS

- Steer clear of beer, wine, spirits, cordials, fruit juices, milk shakes, fizzy drinks, hot
  chocolates, oat milk and rice milk.

What Can I Eat?

Foods You CAN Eat

Below is a list of foods you CAN eat.

- All meats including beef, chicken, lamb, pork and turkey. Avoid breaded and battered meat products.
- Fresh fish such as tuna, haddock, cod, anchovies, salmon, trout, sardines, herring and sole. Shellfish such as prawns, mussels and crab. Avoid breaded or battered fish products.
- Eggs
- Tofu
- Nuts inc. peanut butter, cashew butter and almond butter
- Seeds

FATS

- Butter
- Coconut Oil
- Olive Oil
- Ghee
- Full-fat diary produce; cheeses, Greek yogurt, sour cream, clotted cream, mascarpone, crème fraîche, fresh cream

FRUIT – Maximum 2 pieces of low sugar fruit per day

- Apples
- Apricots
- Bananas
- Blackberries
- Blackcurrants
- Blueberries
- Cherries

- Grapefruit
- Kiwi
- Kumquat
- Lemons
- Limes
- Melon
- Oranges
- Peaches
- Pears
- Plums
- Pomegranate
- Raspberries
- Redcurrants
- Strawberries

VEGETABLES

- Avocados
- Asparagus
- Aubergine (Eggplant)
- Bean sprouts
- Broccoli
- Broad Beans
- Brussels Sprouts
- Cabbage
- Cauliflower
- Celery
- Courgette (Zucchini)
- Cucumber

- Kale
- Leeks
- Lettuce
- Mushrooms
- Pak Choi (Bok choy)
- Peppers (Bell peppers)
- Radish
- Root veg; such as parsnips, beetroots and carrots, in moderation as they have a higher carbohydrate content
- Runner Beans
- Spinach
- Spring Onions (Scallions)
- Olives
- Onions
- Rocket (Arugula)
- Watercress

DRINKS

- Tea
- Coffee
- Green Tea
- Water
- Almond Milk
- Soya Milk

DRESSINGS & CONDIMENTS

- Fresh herbs and spices

Tips On Cooking For One

- Make the most of your freezer and when buying packs of meat, separate it into portions and store them in sealable bags in the freezer. Chicken breasts stored individually won't clump together and mince can be shaped into meatballs or burgers ahead of time and frozen until you need them so there is zero waste.

- You can multiply the quantities to make larger batches of your favourite dishes, ready to be defrosted when you need them.

- When using a small amount of a tin or packet of an ingredient the rest can usually be frozen, so you're not wasting what you haven't used. Alternatively, if you store leftovers in the fridge, try experimenting and adding it to omelettes, curries and casseroles and coming up with new and exciting dishes. This works really well for leftover meats and cooked vegetables.

- Milk, cheese and other dairy products can be frozen which broadens your store cupboard ingredients and means you don't have to make a trip to the shops to pull together a recipe. Double cream (heavy cream) and crème fraîche can also be frozen and added to sauces. (Single cream has a lower fat content and tends to be more watery once defrosted). Try freezing it in ice cube trays as containers can crack during freezing so it prevents leakage and mess. Give it a good stir during thawing in case it separates, but when added to a recipe it combines well.

- If you've over-bought fruit and it's about to over-ripen you can freeze it and add it to smoothies so you don't have to throw it away.

- Frozen vegetables are a quick and handy ingredient to make soups.

- As a general rule, the higher the fat content the better food freezes. Grated (shredded) cheese and butter make great freezer essentials.

- Avoid freezing egg-based sauces which can curdle.

- A tablespoon of chopped fresh herbs can be frozen with a little water in ice cube trays and you can throw them into a soup, stew or casserole.

- Label your freezer bags and storage containers so you know exactly what they contain, otherwise you can forget what you stored.

- Make sure foods are well wrapped to prevent freezer burn.

Breakfast Recipes

Pear & Cucumber Smoothie

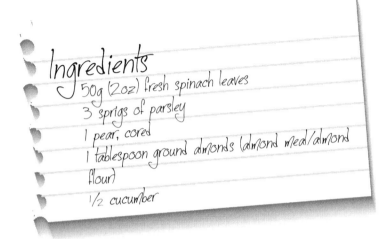

Ingredients
- 50g (2oz) fresh spinach leaves
- 3 sprigs of parsley
- 1 pear, cored
- 1 tablespoon ground almonds (almond meal/almond flour)
- 1/2 cucumber

SERVES 1

212 calories per serving

Method

Place all of the ingredients into a blender and process until smooth. Drink straight away.

Cucumber, Lemon & Coconut Refresher

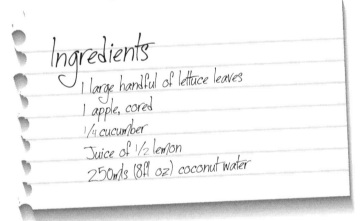

Ingredients
- 1 large handful of lettuce leaves
- 1 apple, cored
- 1/4 cucumber
- Juice of 1/2 lemon
- 250mls (8fl oz) coconut water

SERVES 1

124 calories per serving

Method

Place all of the ingredients into a blender and blitz until smooth. Serve straight away.

Pink Grapefruit & Turmeric Smoothie

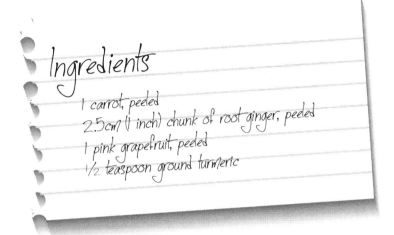

Ingredients

1 carrot, peeled
2.5cm (1 inch) chunk of root ginger, peeled
1 pink grapefruit, peeled
½ teaspoon ground turmeric

**SERVES
1**

167
calories
per serving

Method

Place all of the ingredients into a blender with sufficient water to just cover the ingredients. Blitz until smooth. Serve with a few ice cubes and enjoy.

Peanut Butter & Banana Smoothie

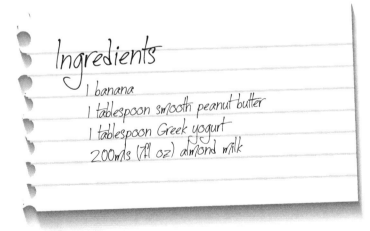

Ingredients

1 banana
1 tablespoon smooth peanut butter
1 tablespoon Greek yogurt
200mls (7fl oz) almond milk

**SERVES
1**

258
calories
per serving

Method

Place all the ingredients into a blender and process until smooth and creamy. Serve with a few ice cubes and drink straight away.

Carrot & Celery Cleanser

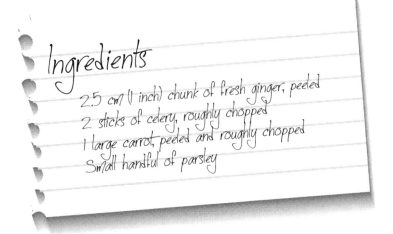

Ingredients

2.5 cm (1 inch) chunk of fresh ginger, peeled
2 sticks of celery, roughly chopped
1 large carrot, peeled and roughly chopped
Small handful of parsley

SERVES 1

44
calories
per serving

Method

Place all of the ingredients into a blender and blitz until smooth.

Nutty Kale Smoothie

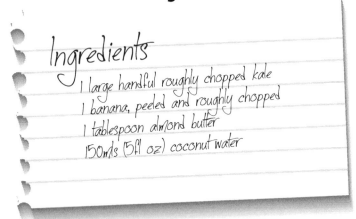

Ingredients

1 large handful roughly chopped kale
1 banana, peeled and roughly chopped
1 tablespoon almond butter
150mls (5fl oz) coconut water

SERVES 1

224
calories
per serving

Method

Place all of the ingredients in a blender and process until smooth.

Tomato & Ginger Smoothie

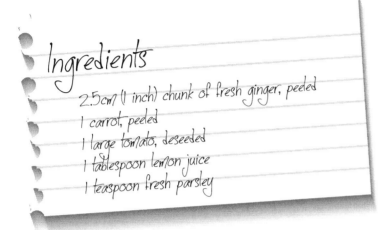

Ingredients

2.5cm (1 inch) chunk of fresh ginger, peeled
1 carrot, peeled
1 large tomato, deseeded
1 tablespoon lemon juice
1 teaspoon fresh parsley

SERVES 1

49
calories
per serving

Method

Place all of the ingredients into a blender with just enough water to cover them. Blitz until smooth. Serve with ice cubes.

Kale & Grapefruit Smoothie

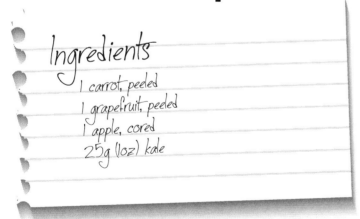

Ingredients

1 carrot, peeled
1 grapefruit, peeled
1 apple, cored
25g (1oz) kale

SERVES 1

132
calories
per serving

Method

Place all of the ingredients into a blender and process until smooth.

Coffee & Almond Smoothie

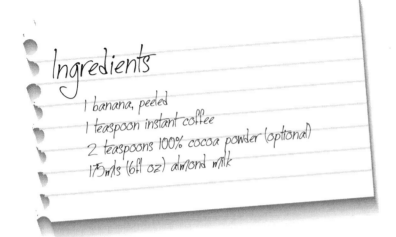

Ingredients

1 banana, peeled
1 teaspoon instant coffee
2 teaspoons 100% cocoa powder (optional)
175mls (6fl oz) almond milk

**SERVES
1**

141
calories
per serving

Method

Place all of the ingredients into a blender and process until smooth. Serve with a few ice cubes.

Apple, Spinach & Seed Smoothie

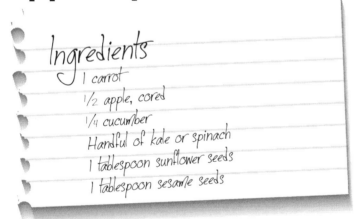

Ingredients

1 carrot
1/2 apple, cored
1/4 cucumber
Handful of kale or spinach
1 tablespoon sunflower seeds
1 tablespoon sesame seeds

**SERVES
1**

243
calories
per serving

Method

Place all the ingredients into a blender and add around a cup of water. Blitz until smooth. You can add a little extra water if it's too thick.

Coconut & Chocolate Muesli

Ingredients

200g (7oz) unsweetened coconut flakes
75g (3oz) cashew nuts, chopped
75g (3oz) almonds, chopped
50g (2oz) hazelnuts, chopped
25g (1oz) cacao nibs
2 tablespoons chia seeds
2 tablespoons 100% cocoa powder
1 teaspoon ground cinnamon
Pinch of salt

MAKES 6
servings

428
calories
per serving

Method

Place all of the ingredients into a large bowl and mix well. Store the muesli in an airtight container until you're ready to use it. Serve with milk or a dollop of yogurt.

Chilli, Bacon & Egg Mug Muffin

Ingredients

1 rasher of bacon, cooked and chopped (or ham)
2 eggs
1/2 teaspoon butter
Pinch of chilli flakes

SERVES 1

224 calories per serving

Method

Crack the eggs into a large mug and beat them. Add in the butter, bacon (or ham if you're using) and chilli flakes and mix well. Place the mug in a microwave and cook on full power for 30 seconds. Stir and return it to the microwave for another 30 seconds, stir and cook for another 30-60 seconds or until the egg is set. Enjoy your eggs straight from the mug. Experiment with your favourite combinations, chicken, sausage, prawns, cheese, spring onions (scallions), tomatoes, peppers and herbs. This makes a great, quick breakfast or an anytime-of-day snack.

Peanut Butter & Cinnamon Yogurt

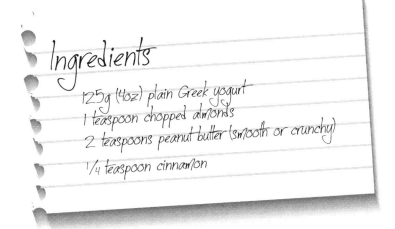

Ingredients

125g (4oz) plain Greek yogurt
1 teaspoon chopped almonds
2 teaspoons peanut butter (smooth or crunchy)
1/4 teaspoon cinnamon

SERVES 1

235
calories
per serving

Method

Place the yogurt in a serving bowl and stir in the peanut butter and cinnamon, mixing them well. Sprinkle with chopped almonds and enjoy.

Apple & Cashew Nut Crunch

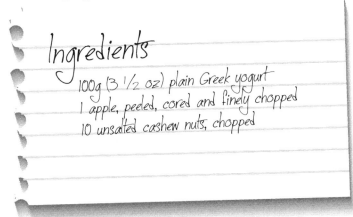

Ingredients

100g (3 1/2 oz) plain Greek yogurt
1 apple, peeled, cored and finely chopped
10 unsalted cashew nuts, chopped

SERVES 1

241
calories
per serving

Method

Stir half of the chopped apple into the yogurt. Using a glass, place a layer of yogurt with a sprinkling of apple and a sprinkling of cashews, followed by another layer of the same until you reach the top of the glass. Garnish with cashew pieces.

Ham & Poached Eggs

Ingredients

2 slices of cooked ham
1 large egg
1 teaspoon white wine vinegar

**SERVES
1**

127
calories
per serving

Method

Boil some water in a large saucepan and add the vinegar to the water. Stir the hot water and gently crack an egg into the middle of the water. Cook for around 3 minutes or until the egg has set. Serve the ham slices onto a plate. Remove the egg using a slotted spoon and allow it to drain for a few seconds. Serve the egg onto the ham slices. Eat immediately. This makes a great breakfast or lunch and will keep you satisfied without feeling too full.

Quinoa & Pear Porridge

Ingredients

75g (3oz) cooked quinoa
1 small pear, peeled, cored and chopped
120mls (4fl oz) almond milk
Pinch of ground cinnamon

**SERVES
1**

145
calories
per serving

Method

Place all of the ingredients into a saucepan, warm it gently for around 7 minutes. Serve with a sprinkling of cinnamon and extra almond milk if you wish.

Basil & Parmesan Scramble

SERVES 1

211
calories
per serving

Ingredients

2 eggs
1 teaspoon crème fraîche
1 tablespoon grated Parmesan cheese
4 fresh basil leaves, chopped
1 teaspoon butter
Sea salt
Freshly ground black pepper

Method

Break the eggs into a bowl, whisk them and add in the cheese, crème fraiche and basil leaves. Season with salt and pepper. Heat the butter in a frying pan. Pour in the egg mixture and stir constantly until the eggs are scrambled and set. Serve and eat immediately.

Tomato & Spinach Scramble

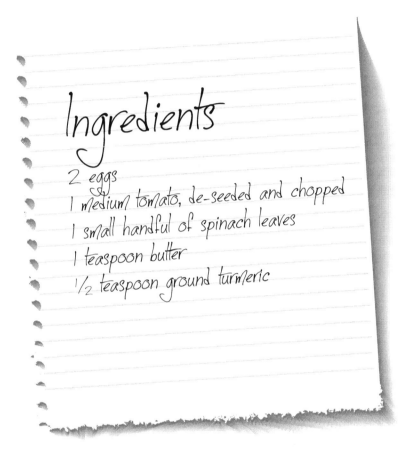

Ingredients

2 eggs
1 medium tomato, de-seeded and chopped
1 small handful of spinach leaves
1 teaspoon butter
½ teaspoon ground turmeric

SERVES 1

189
calories
per serving

Method

Break the eggs into a bowl, sprinkle in the turmeric and mix well. Heat the butter in a frying pan, add in the spinach and tomatoes and cook for 2 minutes. Pour in the beaten eggs and stir constantly until the eggs are scrambled and completely cooked.

Lunch
Recipes

Quick Red Pepper Soup

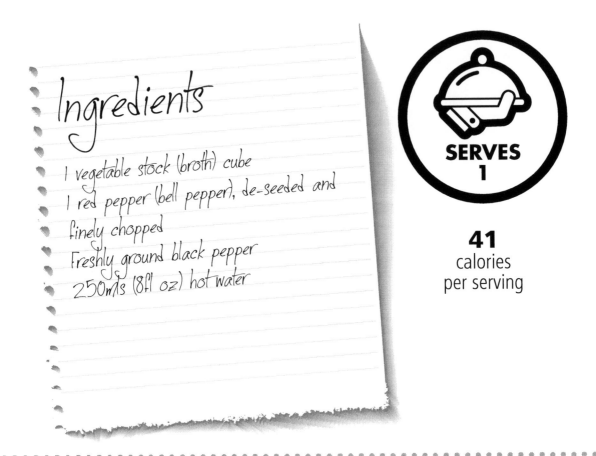

Ingredients

1 vegetable stock (broth) cube
1 red pepper (bell pepper), de-seeded and finely chopped
Freshly ground black pepper
250mls (8fl oz) hot water

**SERVES
1**

41
calories
per serving

Method

Place the hot water, stock (broth) cube and red pepper (bell pepper) into a saucepan.
Bring it to the boil, reduce the heat and simmer for 5 minutes. Using a hand blender or
food processor whizz the soup until smooth. Season with pepper. Eat straight away.
You can even stir in a teaspoon of crème fraiche to make it rich and creamy.

Carrot & Tomato Soup

Ingredients

400g (14oz) tin of chopped tomatoes
1 carrot, peeled and chopped
½ onion, peeled and chopped
Pinch of mixed herbs
1 teaspoon olive oil

**SERVES
1**

173
calories
per serving

Method

Heat the oil in a saucepan, add the onion and cook for 3 minutes. Add in the carrot and cook for 2 minutes. Stir in the chopped tomatoes and add around a cup of warm water or enough to cover the ingredients. Simmer gently for around 15 minutes or until the carrots have softened stirring occasionally and add some extra hot water if required. Stir in the mixed herbs. Use a stick blender or cool the soup slightly and place it in a food processor until smooth. Serve and enjoy.

Chicken & Mushroom Soup

Ingredients

100g (3½ oz) cooked chicken, chopped
3 medium mushrooms, finely chopped
2 spring onions (scallions) finely chopped
1 stick of celery, finely chopped
1 teaspoon butter
1 teaspoon fresh parsley, chopped
250mls (8fl oz) chicken stock (broth)
Sea salt
Freshly ground black pepper

**SERVES
1**

212
calories
per serving

Method

Heat the butter in a saucepan, add the mushrooms, celery and spring onions (scallions) and cook for 5 minutes. Pour in the chicken stock (broth) and chopped chicken. Bring it to the boil, reduce the heat and cook for 10 minutes. Stir in the fresh parsley and season with salt and pepper. Serve as it is or blend it until smooth.

Spicy Tomato & Basil Soup

Ingredients

400g (14oz) tin of chopped tomatoes
5 fresh basil leaves, chopped
1 teaspoon tomato purée (paste)
1/4 courgette (zucchini), chopped
200mls hot water
1 vegetable stock (broth) cube
Pinch of chilli flakes (or to taste)
Freshly ground black pepper

SERVES
1

97
calories
per serving

Method

Place all the ingredients into a saucepan. Bring it to the boil, reduce the heat and simmer for 20 minutes, stirring occasionally and adding more hot water, if required. Season with black pepper. Using a stick blender or food processor blitz the soup until smooth. Serve and eat immediately.

Thai Crab Soup

Ingredients

100g (3½ oz) cooked crab meat
1 teaspoon Thai red curry paste
½ green pepper (bell pepper), chopped
75mls (3fl oz) coconut milk
150mls (5fl oz) vegetable stock (broth)
1 teaspoon fish sauce
1 teaspoon fresh coriander (cilantro), chopped
1 teaspoon olive oil

SERVES 1

303
calories
per serving

Method

Heat the olive oil in a frying pan, add the green pepper (bell pepper) and cook for 4 minutes. Stir in the curry paste and pour in the stock (broth) and cook for 1 minute. Add in the fish sauce, crab meat and coconut milk and cook for around 10 minutes. Stir in the coriander (cilantro) and make sure the soup is warmed through.

Chorizo & Sprouts

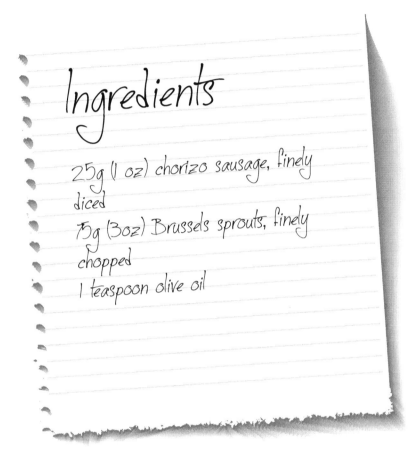

Ingredients

25g (1 oz) chorizo sausage, finely diced

75g (3oz) Brussels sprouts, finely chopped

1 teaspoon olive oil

**SERVES
1**

187
calories
per serving

Method

Heat the oil in a frying pan, add the chorizo sausage to the pan and cook for 2 minutes. Add in the Brussels sprouts. Cook for around 5 minutes, or until the sprouts have softened and the sausage is warmed through. Serve and eat straight away.

Spiced Prawns & Lentils

Ingredients

100g (3½ oz) shelled raw prawns (shrimps)

75g (3oz) cooked puy lentils

50g (2oz) spinach leaves

1 spring onion (scallion), chopped

¼ teaspoon chilli flakes (or to taste)

½ teaspoon ground coriander (cilantro)

½ teaspoon ground turmeric

½ teaspoon ground cumin

1 teaspoon apple cider vinegar

2 teaspoons olive oil

SERVES 1

291 calories per serving

Method

Heat the olive oil in a saucepan, add the lentils, spring onion (scallion), vinegar, cumin, turmeric and coriander (cilantro). Stir in the prawns (shrimps) and cook until they become pink throughout and are completely cooked. Scatter the spinach leaves on a plate and serve the prawns and lentils on top. Serve and eat straight away.

Beetroot, Carrot & Coriander Salad

Ingredients

1 carrot, peeled

3 cooked baby beetroot (unsweetened)

2 radishes, topped and tailed

1 tablespoon fresh coriander (cilantro), chopped

1 teaspoon olive oil

SERVES 1

122 calories per serving

Method

Grate (shred) the carrot into a bowl then do the same with the beetroot and radishes. Add in the olive oil and coriander (cilantro) and mix the ingredients well.

Roast Cauliflower Couscous

Ingredients

½ small cauliflower
1 teaspoon olive oil
Sea salt

**SERVES
1**

76
calories
per serving

Method

Grate (shred) the cauliflower or alternatively blitz it in a food processor until it resembles a grain. Stir in the olive oil and season with salt. Scatter the cauliflower on a baking sheet. Transfer it to the oven and cook at 200C/400F for 15 minutes or until the cauliflower is soft and golden. This is such a versatile dish which is a great carbohydrate alternative to many dishes. It's worthwhile doubling your quantities and making a large batch which can be stored in the fridge until you're ready to use it.

Alternatives to plain roast cauliflower couscous are endless – try experimenting with herbs, spices or adding flaked almonds or pine nuts.

Cauliflower Mash

Ingredients

½ small cauliflower, broken into florets
1 teaspoon butter
25mls (1fl oz) milk
Sea salt
Freshly ground black pepper

**SERVES
1**

86
calories
per serving

Method

Steam the cauliflower for around 10 minutes or until it becomes tender. Transfer it to a food processor or hand blender and add in the butter, milk, salt and pepper. Blitz it until smooth and creamy. Serve as an alternative to mashed potatoes. Make a larger batch and store it in the fridge as a great time-saving carb alternative.

Gazpacho

Ingredients

2 tomatoes, de-seeded and chopped
1 red pepper (bell pepper), de-seeded and chopped
1 clove of garlic, chopped
1/2 cucumber, peeled and chopped
1/4 teaspoon chilli flakes
1 teaspoon olive oil
1 tablespoon apple cider vinegar

SERVES 1

122 calories per serving

Method

Place all of the ingredients into a blender and process until smooth and creamy. Chill the soup in the fridge for an hour before serving.

Parma Ham & Mozzarella Salad With Kiwi Dressing

Ingredients

50g (2oz) strawberries
50g (2oz) mozzarella
2 slices Parma ham
3 walnuts, chopped
1 handful of fresh basil, chopped

FOR THE DRESSING
1 kiwi fruit
Zest and juice of ½ lime
1 teaspoon olive oil
1 teaspoon vinegar
Sea salt
Freshly ground black pepper

SERVES 1

362
calories
per serving

Method

Place the kiwi fruit into a blender and process until smooth. Mix in the olive oil, vinegar and lime. Season with salt and pepper. Scatter the Parma ham, mozzarella, strawberries, basil and walnuts on a plate and spoon the kiwi dressing over the top.

Cream of Celery Soup

Ingredients

4 stalks of celery, chopped
1 clove of garlic, chopped
1 tablespoon fresh parsley, chopped
½ onion, chopped
250mls (8fl oz) vegetable stock (broth)
1 tablespoon crème fraîche
2 teaspoons olive oil

SERVES 1

144 calories per serving

Method

Heat the olive oil in a saucepan, add the onion, celery and garlic and cook for 5 minutes until the vegetables have softened. Add in the vegetable stock (broth), bring it to the boil, reduce the heat and simmer for 15 minutes. Stir in the parsley and crème fraiche. Using a food processor or hand blender process the soup until smooth and creamy. Serve and eat straight away.

Broccoli & Pesto Soup

Ingredients

3 large broccoli florets

1 vegetable stock (broth) cube

1 teaspoon pesto sauce

2 teaspoons crème fraîche

360mls (12fl oz) warm water

Freshly ground black pepper

SERVES
1

61
calories
per serving

Method

Pour the water into a saucepan, add the broccoli and cook for around 8-10 minutes or until the broccoli is soft. Add in the stock (broth) cube and stir until it dissolves. Using a hand blender or food processor whizz the soup until smooth. Stir in the pesto sauce and crème fraîche. Season with black pepper and serve.

Chicken & Avocado Salad

Ingredients

1 chicken breast
1 teaspoon olive oil
1 teaspoon smoked paprika

FOR THE SALAD
1/2 avocado, flesh and stone removed
1 teaspoon olive oil
1 teaspoon red wine vinegar
1 tablespoon fresh parsley, chopped
1 large tomato, chopped
2 spring onions (scallions), chopped

**SERVES
1**

432
calories
per serving

Method

Coat the chicken in the olive oil and sprinkle on the paprika. Place it under a grill and cook for around 14 minutes, until completely cooked, turning once halfway through. Place the oil, vinegar and parsley in a bowl and mix well. Add in the avocado, tomato and spring onions (scallions) and coat them in the dressing. Serve the salad onto a plate. Slice the cooked chicken breast and serve on top of the salad.

Grilled Asparagus With Herby Goat's Cheese Slice

Ingredients

125g (4oz) asparagus spears, trimmed
25g (1oz) slice of Goat's cheese
1 teaspoon olive oil
1 teaspoon chives

**SERVES
1**

153
calories
per serving

Method

Coat the asparagus spears in olive oil and place them under a hot grill. Cook for around 5 minutes, turning half-way through. Place the asparagus on a serving plate and add the slice of Goat's cheese to the top. Return it to the grill and cook until the cheese becomes soft. Sprinkle with chives. Serve and eat straight away.

Prawn & Egg Layered Salad

Ingredients

100g (3½ oz) peeled, cooked prawns
1 egg
1 Baby Gem lettuce, finely chopped
1 tablespoon sweetcorn
1 carrot, grated (shredded)
½ small cucumber, diced
1 tablespoon mayonnaise
1 teaspoon tomato purée (paste)
Dash of Tabasco sauce
Wedge of lemon

**SERVES
1**

330
calories
per serving

Method

Mix together the mayonnaise, tomato purée (paste) and Tabasco sauce. Place the egg in hot water, bring it to the boil and cook for 7-8 minutes. Run it under cold water and when sufficiently cool, peel off the shell and slice it. Place the chopped lettuce in a bowl, add a layer of sweetcorn then separate layers of cucumber, carrot, egg and prawns. Spoon the dressing over the top and serve with the wedge of lemon.

Creamy Shitake Mushroom Omelette

Ingredients

2 large eggs, beaten
50g (2oz) shitake mushrooms, sliced
1 tablespoon crème fraîche
1 teaspoon olive oil
Sea salt
Freshly ground black pepper

SERVES 1

191
calories
per serving

Method

Heat the oil in a frying pan, add the mushrooms and cook for 5 minutes until they soften. Stir in the crème fraîche and season with salt and pepper. Remove the mixture, set it aside and keep it warm. Pour the beaten egg into the frying pan and allow it to set and cook until the underside is slightly golden. Serve the omelette onto a plate and spoon the creamy mushroom mixture onto one side. Fold the other side of the omelette over the top. Eat immediately.

Quick Miso Soup

SERVES 1

82 calories per serving

Ingredients

50g (2oz) tofu, diced
2 spring onions (scallions), chopped
2 tablespoons miso paste
300mls (10fl oz) vegetable stock (broth)

Method

Mix 2 tablespoons of the vegetable (broth) stock with the miso paste. Set aside. Heat the remaining stock (broth) in a saucepan, add in the diced tofu and cook it for around 10 minutes. Sprinkle in the spring onions (scallions) and stir in the miso paste. Serve immediately.

Tuna & Mixed Bean Salad

Ingredients

125g (4oz) tuna in brine, drained
100g (3½ oz) tinned mixed beans
2 teaspoons olive oil
1 tablespoon lemon juice
1 clove of garlic, chopped
1 spring onion (scallion) chopped
2 teaspoons fresh basil, chopped
Sea salt
Freshly ground black pepper

**SERVES
1**

324
calories
per serving

Method

Place the beans in a bowl and add in the oil, garlic, spring onion, lemon juice and basil and mix well. Season with salt and pepper. Add in the tuna flakes and combine with the other ingredients. Serve and eat immediately.

Mushroom & Fennel Quinoa

Ingredients

100g (3½oz) cooked quinoa
5 medium mushrooms, chopped
1 clove of garlic, chopped
1 tablespoon fresh basil, chopped
¼ bulb of fennel, finely sliced
1 tablespoon olive oil
1 tablespoon apple cider vinegar
Sea salt
Freshly ground black pepper

**SERVES
1**

250
calories
per serving

Method

Heat the oil in a frying pan, add in the mushrooms, fennel and garlic and cook for 5 minutes. Stir in the cooked quinoa, vinegar and basil. Season with salt and pepper.

Quick Cauliflower Cheese

Ingredients

- 100g (3½oz) cauliflower, broken into florets
- 25g (1oz) cheddar cheese, grated (shredded)
- Pinch of mixed spice
- Sea salt
- Freshly ground black pepper

SERVES 1

133 calories per serving

Method

Place the cauliflower florets into a steamer and cook for around 10 minutes or until it has softened. Transfer the cauliflower to a heatproof dish. Sprinkle on a little mixed spice and season with salt and pepper. Scatter the grated cheese on top and place it under a hot grill (broiler) for a few minutes until the cheese begins to bubble.

Quinoa Tabbouleh Salad

Ingredients

- 100g (3½ oz) cooked quinoa
- 2 spring onions (scallions), chopped
- 1 small handful of fresh coriander (cilantro)
- 1 small handful of fresh mint
- 1 large tomato
- ¼ cucumber, chopped
- flesh of ½ avocado, diced
- 1 tablespoon lemon juice
- 2 teaspoons olive oil
- 1 teaspoon apple cider vinegar
- Sea salt
- Freshly ground black pepper

SERVES 1

370 calories per serving

Method

In a small bowl, mix together the olive oil, lemon juice, vinegar, salt and pepper. Place all the remaining ingredients into a large bowl and mix well. Pour in the dressing mixture and stir well. Chill before serving.

Parma Ham, Fennel & Rocket Salad

Ingredients

50g (2oz) Parma ham, sliced
2 slices of fennel, finely sliced
1 large handful of rocket (arugula) leaves, washed
1 teaspoon lemon juice
2 teaspoons olive oil
Sea salt
Freshly ground black pepper

**SERVES
1**

206
calories
per serving

Method

Pour the olive oil and lemon juice in a bowl and mix well. Season with salt and pepper. Add the rocket (arugula) leaves and fennel slices and coat them in the oil. Serve the rocket salad and add the Parma ham slices on top. Enjoy!

Radish & Salmon Salad

Ingredients

100g (3 ½ oz) smoked salmon, roughly chopped

6 radishes, topped, tailed and sliced

2 spring onions (scallions), chopped

Zest and juice of 1 orange

1 teaspoon olive oil

1 teaspoon apple cider vinegar

Sea salt

Freshly ground black pepper

SERVES 1

242 calories per serving

Method

In a bowl, combine the orange juice, vinegar and olive oil. Add the radishes, spring onions (scallions) and salmon and coat them in the oil mixture. Season with salt and pepper. Eat immediately.

Dinner Recipes

Chicken Stew

Ingredients

- 75g (3oz) cannellini beans
- 2 stalks of celery, chopped
- 1 skinless chicken breast, chopped
- 1 carrot
- 1/2 onion, chopped
- 1/2 teaspoon mixed herbs
- 1 tablespoon fresh parsley, chopped
- 250mls (8fl oz) chicken stock (broth)
- 1 teaspoon olive oil
- Sea salt
- Pepper

SERVES 1

378 calories per serving

Method

Heat the oil in a saucepan, add the chicken breast and cook for 3-4 minutes. Add in the onion, carrot, celery and stock (broth), reduce the heat and simmer for 20 minutes, making sure the chicken is completely cooked. Stir in the beans and mixed herbs and warm the stew thoroughly. Season with salt and pepper and sprinkle in the parsley.

Steak Béarnaise

Ingredients

150g (5oz) sirloin steak
2 tablespoons crème fraiche
1 tablespoon red wine vinegar
2 teaspoons wholegrain mustard
1 tablespoon fresh tarragon, chopped
2 handfuls of green salad leaves
1 tablespoon olive oil
Sea salt
Freshly ground black pepper

**SERVES
1**

436
calories
per serving

Method

Season the steak with salt and pepper. Heat the olive oil in a frying pan and add the steak. Cook for around 1 ½ to 2 minutes on each side or longer depending on how well cooked you like it. Remove the steak from the pan. Reduce the heat and add in the vinegar. Stir in the mustard, crème fraiche and stir. Scatter in the tarragon and stir well. Serve the steak onto a plate and pour the sauce over the top. Serve with green salad leaves.

Pesto Roast Vegetables

Ingredients

**SERVES
1**

1 small courgette (zucchini), chopped

1 red pepper (bell pepper), chopped

1 medium tomato, chopped

3 florets of broccoli, roughly chopped

1/2 teaspoon mixed herbs

2 teaspoons pesto sauce

2 teaspoons olive oil

214
calories
per serving

Method

Place all of the ingredients, apart from the pesto, into a large ovenproof dish and mix them well. Place them in the oven and cook at 200C/400F for 30 minutes, stirring the ingredients half-way through cooking. Remove from the oven and stir in the pesto sauce, coating all the vegetables well. Serve as an alternative to potatoes, pasta and rice.

Creamy Fish Curry

Ingredients

125g (4oz) cod
25g (1oz) creamed coconut, chopped
2 cardamom pods
1 small onion, finely chopped
1 clove of garlic, finely chopped
1 small red chilli, chopped
1 teaspoon curry powder
1/2 teaspoon garam masala
1/2 teaspoon turmeric
1/4 teaspoon ground ginger
4 tablespoons warm water
2 teaspoons olive oil

SERVES 1

411 calories per serving

Method

Heat the olive oil in a frying pan, add the onion, ginger, garlic, chilli and stir constantly for a few seconds. Add in the turmeric, cardamom pods, garam masala and curry powder and 4 tablespoons of warm water and cook for 2 minutes, constantly stirring. Add in the cod and cook gently for around 10 minutes. Add the creamed coconut to the mixture and stir until it has melted. Serve and enjoy. Can be served with cauliflower rice or a leafy green salad.

Blackberry & Apple Pork

Ingredients

25g (1oz) fresh blackberries

12g (½ oz) butter

1 large pork steak

1 apple, cored, peeled and chopped

1 small handful of fresh baby spinach leaves

1 small handful of rocket (arugula) leaves

3 tablespoons of water

1 tablespoon fresh orange juice

Pinch of cinnamon

SERVES 1

306
calories
per serving

Method

Place the blackberries, apple, cinnamon and orange juice in a saucepan with 3 tablespoons of water. Cover the saucepan and warm them slowly until the apples have softened. Check if the liquid is evaporating too quickly and add a little extra water if required. Heat the butter in a frying pan, add the pork and cook for around 4 minutes on each side until it's cooked through. Scatter the spinach and rocket (arugula) leaves on a plate. Serve the pork steak onto the leaves and spoon the apple and blackberry mixture over the top. Eat immediately.

Garlic & Caper Chicken

Ingredients

1 chicken breast
1/2 teaspoon salt
1/4 teaspoon dried dill
1 clove of garlic
2 teaspoons butter
2 teaspoons capers, drained
1 tablespoon lemon juice
25mls (1fl oz) double cream (heavy cream)

SERVES
1

347
calories
per serving

Method

Place the lemon juice, salt, dill and garlic in a bowl. Add the chicken and coat it in the mixture. Heat the butter in a frying pan. Add the chicken and cook for 10-15 minutes turning once halfway through cooking. Remove the chicken breast and keep it warm. Pour the cream into the frying pan and warm it gently. Stir in the capers. Serve the chicken and pour the sauce over the top. Can be served with cauliflower rice or roast vegetables.

Chicken & Halloumi Skewers

SERVES 1

496
calories
per serving

Ingredients

75g (3oz) halloumi cheese, cut into chunks

4 cherry tomatoes

1 chicken breast, cut into chunks

1 teaspoon ground coriander (cilantro)

½ red pepper (bell pepper), cut into chunks

¼ teaspoon chilli flakes

2 teaspoons Greek yogurt

Pinch of sea salt

Method

In a bowl, mix together the yogurt, coriander (cilantro) and chilli and season with a pinch of salt. Add the chicken to the marinade and allow it to marinate for 30 minutes or longer if you can. Thread the chicken chunks onto skewers, alternating between the red pepper (bell pepper), tomatoes and halloumi. Place them under a hot grill and cook for 12-15 minutes or until completely cooked, turning them half way through to ensure even cooking.

Mushroom & Hazelnut Peppers

Ingredients

- 6 medium mushrooms, finely chopped
- 1 red pepper (bell pepper), halved and seeds removed
- 1 clove of garlic, chopped
- 10 hazelnuts, chopped
- 1 teaspoon fresh chives, chopped
- 1 teaspoon smooth peanut butter
- 2 teaspoons olive oil
- Sea salt
- Freshly ground black pepper

SERVES 1

220 calories per serving

Method

Coat the peppers in a teaspoon of olive oil, place them on a baking sheet and bake in the oven at 180C/360F for 5 minutes. Heat a teaspoon of olive oil in a frying pan, add the mushrooms and garlic and cook until the mushrooms soften. Place the mushrooms, hazelnuts, chives and peanut butter into a bowl and mix well. Season with salt and pepper. Remove the peppers from the oven and spoon the mushroom mixture into them. Return them to the oven and bake for 15 minutes. Serve and eat straight away.

Salmon & Creamy Herby Greens

Ingredients

25g (1oz) frozen peas

25g (1oz) broad beans

1 salmon fillet, approx. 100g (3½ oz) without skin

1 leek, finely chopped

1 tablespoon crème fraîche

1 small handful of chives, chopped

100mls (3½fl oz) vegetable stock (broth)

1 teaspoon olive oil

Sea salt

Freshly ground black pepper

SERVES 1

381
calories
per serving

Method

Heat the oil in a large, deep frying pan with a lid. Cook the leek for 5-10 minutes until soft but not coloured, then pour in the stock (broth). Simmer for a few minutes until reduced slightly then add the crème fraîche and season. Cook for 1 min more. Tip in the peas and beans, nestle in the salmon fillets and then turn down to a simmer and cover. Cook for 12-15 minutes depending on the thickness of the salmon, until cooked through. Sprinkle on the chives and serve with mashed potato, if you like.

Mustard Pork & Green Beans

Ingredients

75g (3oz) green beans
15g (½ oz) cheddar cheese, grated
1 large pork chop
½ teaspoon mustard
½ teaspoon crème fraîche

**SERVES
1**

346
calories
per serving

Method

Mix together the mustard, crème fraîche and cheese. Spread the mixture on top of the pork chop. Heat the oven to 200C/400F. Place the chop in an ovenproof dish and place it in the oven and cook for 15 minutes. In the meantime, steam the green beans for 5 minutes until softened. Serve the green beans on a plate and place the cooked pork on top.

Ginger Chicken

Ingredients

2.5cm (1 inch) chunk of fresh ginger root

1 chicken breast

1 clove of garlic

1 tablespoon tomato purée

1/4 teaspoon cayenne pepper

1/2 onion, chopped

1 teaspoon vinegar

2 teaspoons olive oil

2 teaspoons soy sauce

1/2 cup of water

SERVES 1

328
calories
per serving

Method

Heat the olive oil in a frying pan, add the chicken and cook for 3 minutes. Remove it from the pan, set it aside and keep it warm. Add the garlic, ginger and onion to the pan and cook for 3 minutes. In the meantime, mix together the soy sauce, tomato purée, vinegar, cayenne pepper and water in a bowl. Return the chicken to the frying pan and pour in the tomato mixture. Heat the sauce thoroughly.

Slow Cooked Cod With Pea Purée

SERVES 1

236 calories per serving

Ingredients

125g (4oz) peas
1 cod fillet, approx. 125g (4oz)
1 tablespoon crème fraîche
3 fresh mint leaves
100mls (3½ fl oz) vegetable stock (broth)

Method

Pour the stock (broth) into the bottom of a slow cooker and add in the peas. Place the fish on top of the peas. Place the lid on the cooker and cook on high for 1 ½ to 2 hours or until the fish is completely cooked. Remove the fish and keep it warm. Remove the peas from the cooker using a slotted spoon and discard the stock (broth). Place the peas in a food processor, add the crème fraîche and mint and blitz until it becomes a smooth puree. Serve the cod onto a plate alongside the puree. To make best use of the cooking time you can easily double up the quantities and make extra with this recipe.

Lamb & Mushroom Slow Cooked Casserole

SERVES 1

331 calories per serving

Ingredients

125g (4oz) lamb steak, cut into chunks

75g (3oz) button mushrooms

50g (2oz) shallots, peeled

2 large tomatoes, chopped

1 carrot, peeled and chopped

1 clove of garlic

1 teaspoon tomato purée (paste)

1 teaspoon soy sauce

1 sprig of rosemary

100mls (3½ fl oz) warm lamb or vegetable stock (broth)

Method

Place all of the ingredients into a slow cooker and add the lid. Cook on a low heat for around 6 hours. As with the previous slow cooker recipe, if longer cooking time puts you off you can easily multiply the quantities in this recipe and store/freeze the leftovers.

Grilled Pork, Apple & Blue Cheese

Ingredients

25g (1oz) blue cheese
2 thick slices of apple
1 pork chop
1 large handful of salad leaves

SERVES 1

309 calories per serving

Method

Heat the grill and place the pork chop underneath. Cook for around 15 minutes, turning once halfway through cooking. Place the apple slices on top of the chop and add the cheese on top. Return it to the grill and cook for 2-3 minutes or until the cheese has melted. Serve the chop on a plate alongside the salad leaves

Fennel Chicken & Celeriac Coleslaw

Ingredients

100g (3½ oz) celeriac, peeled and grated (shredded)
1 carrot, grated (shredded)
1 medium chicken breast
½ onion, grated (shredded)
¼ teaspoon fennel seeds
Pinch of chilli flakes
2 teaspoons mayonnaise
1 teaspoon apple cider vinegar
1 teaspoon wholegrain mustard
1 teaspoon olive oil

**SERVES
1**

378
calories
per serving

Method

Place the olive oil, fennel seeds and chilli flakes into a bowl and mix well. Coat the chicken breast in the oil mixture. Place the chicken under a hot grill (broiler) and cook for around 15 minutes until cooked through, turning once halfway through cooking. In the meantime, place the mayonnaise, vinegar and mustard into a bowl and mix well. Add in the onion, carrot and celeriac and mix well. Serve the chicken with the coleslaw alongside.

Chicken, Creamy Beans & Leeks

Ingredients

125g (4oz) cannellini beans
1 tablespoon crème fraîche
1 chicken breast
1 small leek, chopped
1 clove of garlic, chopped
75mls (3fl oz) vegetable stock (broth)
2 teaspoons olive oil
Sea salt
Freshly ground black pepper

**SERVES
1**

437
calories
per serving

Method

Heat a teaspoon of olive oil in a saucepan, add the garlic and leek and cook for 4-5 minutes until softened. Stir in the beans and add in the stock (broth) and cook for 10 minutes. Pour in the crème fraîche. Season with salt and pepper. Warm the mixture until it thickens slightly. In the meantime, heat a teaspoon of olive oil in a frying pan, add the chicken and cook for around 5 minutes on each side or until completely cooked. Serve the creamy bean mixture onto plates and top it off with the chicken fillet. Serve on its own or with a leafy green salad.

Citrus Lamb Skewers

Ingredients

2 lamb steaks, cubed

4 shallots

1 small orange, quartered

1 clove of garlic, chopped

2 teaspoons lemon juice

1/2 teaspoon lemon zest

1/2 teaspoon ground coriander (cilantro)

1/4 teaspoon ground cumin

2 teaspoons apple cider vinegar

1 tablespoon olive oil

SERVES 1

496 calories per serving

Method

Place the garlic, shallots, lemon juice, zest, coriander (cilantro), cumin, vinegar and oil into a bowl and mix well. Add in the lamb pieces and coat them well in the marinade. Allow to sit for at least 30 minutes to absorb the flavour. Thread the lamb, shallots and orange pieces alternately onto skewers. Place the skewers under a hot grill/broiler and cook for 10-12 minutes, turning halfway through cooking, until the lamb is cooked the way you like it.

Salt & Pepper Prawns

Ingredients

200g (7oz) large peeled raw prawns (shrimps)
1/2 teaspoon sea salt
1/4 teaspoon freshly ground black pepper
1/2 teaspoon Szechuan pepper
1/2 teaspoon sesame oil
1/4 teaspoon chilli flakes
1 clove of garlic, crushed
2 spring onions (scallions), finely chopped

**SERVES
1**

181
calories
per serving

Method

Place the salt, black pepper, chilli flakes and Szechuan pepper into a bowl. Heat the oil in a frying pan, add the prawns and garlic and cook until the prawns are completely pink. Sprinkle in the salt and pepper seasoning and mix well. Serve into a bowl, sprinkle with spring onions (scallions) and eat straight away.

Chicken & Creamy Mushroom Sauce

SERVES 1

277
calories
per serving

Ingredients

2 large mushrooms, sliced
1 medium chicken fillet
½ red onion, finely chopped
1 tablespoon crème fraîche
1 teaspoon olive oil
Sea salt
Freshly ground black pepper

Method

Heat the oil in a frying pan, add the chicken and cook for around 4 minutes on each side, until cooked through. Remove the chicken and keep it warm. Add the mushrooms and onion to the pan. Cook until softened. Pour in the crème fraîche and warm it completely. Season with salt and pepper. Serve the chicken and pour the sauce on top.

Scallops & Herby Garlic Butter

Ingredients

100g (4 ½ oz) large scallops, shelled

12g (½ oz) butter

2 teaspoons fresh parsley, finely chopped

1 clove of garlic, finely chopped

1 teaspoon olive oil

1 teaspoon lemon juice

Sea salt

Freshly ground black pepper

**SERVES
1**

251
calories
per serving

Method

Place the olive oil in a frying pan over a high heat. Add the scallops and cook for around
1 minute on either side until they are slightly golden. Transfer to a dish and keep warm.
Drain off any excess liquid from the pan. Gently warm the butter and the garlic for around
1 minute until the butter has melted, add the parsley and lemon juice. Serve the scallops
onto a plate and spoon the garlic butter on top. Season with salt and pepper.

Prawn & Cashew Stir-Fry

Ingredients

8 large king prawns, peeled
2 spring onions (scallions), chopped
2 florets of broccoli, sliced
1 clove of garlic
1 tablespoon cashew nuts, chopped
1 tablespoon coconut chips (unsweetened)
1 teaspoon peanut butter
1/2 green pepper (bell pepper), chopped
1/2 courgette (zucchini), spiralised or finely sliced
2 teaspoons soy sauce
2 tablespoons lemon juice
1 teaspoon sesame oil
Pinch of chilli flakes
Sea salt

**SERVES
1**

322
calories
per serving

Method

Heat the oil in a wok or a large frying pan, add the garlic, spring onions (scallions), courgette (zucchini), broccoli, green pepper (bell pepper), peanut butter, chilli flakes, lemon juice and soy sauce and for around 4 minutes or until the vegetables have softened slightly. Add in the prawns and cook until they are pink throughout. Season with salt. Scatter in the cashews and coconut chips into the stir-fry and mix well. Serve on its own or with cauliflower couscous.

Bacon & Cheeseburger Wrap

Ingredients

125g (4oz) minced steak (ground steak)
2 large romaine lettuce leaves
2 rashers of bacon
1 clove of garlic, chopped
1 teaspoon horseradish
2 slices of cheese

**SERVES
1**

542
calories
per serving

Method

Place the steak mince in a bowl and add in the garlic and horseradish. Combine the ingredients. Shape the mixture into two beef burgers shapes. Place the burgers under a hot grill along with the bacon rashers. Cook the bacon and burgers until done to your liking, turning once half-way through. Lay the lettuce leaves onto a plate and serve the burgers into them. Add the cheese on top of the burgers and a rasher of bacon onto each one. Fold the lettuce leaves around the burgers and eat immediately.

Baked Plaice With Lemon & Herbs

Ingredients

1 plaice fillet
1 teaspoon fresh chives
1 tablespoon fresh parsley
Zest and juice of 1/2 lemon
1 teaspoon capers
1 teaspoon olive oil
Sea salt
Freshly ground black pepper

**SERVES
1**

176
calories
per serving

Method

Cut off a large piece of foil and lay the fish on the foil. Drizzle over the olive oil and sprinkle on the herbs, capers, lemon juice and zest. Season with salt and pepper. Fold the edges of the foil over the fish to create a parcel. Place the parcel on a baking sheet, transfer it to the oven and bake at 190C/375F for around 15 minutes until the fish is completely cooked. Serve with roasted vegetables or a leafy green salad.

Baked Mediterranean Meatballs & Roast Vegetables

Ingredients

150g (5oz) lean minced beef (ground beef)
6 medium mushrooms, chopped
1 large tomato, chopped
1 red pepper (bell pepper), chopped
3 spring onions (scallions), chopped
2 tablespoons fresh basil leaves, chopped
1 clove of garlic, chopped
1 teaspoon olive oil
Sea salt
Freshly ground black pepper

SERVES
1

411
calories
per serving

Method

Place the beef into a bowl and add the garlic and basil. Season with salt and pepper and shape the meat into small balls. Coat an ovenproof dish with a teaspoon of olive oil and place the meat balls in the centre. Place the red pepper (bell pepper), mushrooms, tomato and spring onions (scallions) in the dish. Transfer to the oven and cook at 220C/425F for 10-15 minutes until the meatballs are completely cooked.

Pork & Orange Gremolata

Ingredients

1 pork steak
1 tablespoon fresh orange juice
1 tablespoon red wine vinegar
1 clove of garlic
1 teaspoon olive oil

GREMOLATA
Rind of ½ orange, grated (shredded)
1 tablespoon fresh parsley chopped
1 clove of garlic, crushed

**SERVES
1**

219
calories
per serving

Method

Place the vinegar, orange juice and garlic in a flat dish and add the pork steak, turning it over to coat it in the mixture. Allow to marinate for at least ½ hour. In the meantime, mix all the ingredients for the gremolata in a bowl, cover and set aside. Heat the olive oil in a frying pan, add the pork steak and marinade and cook for around 5 minutes on each side until the juices run clear and it's thoroughly cooked. Serve the pork onto a plate and spoon the gremolata over the top.

Fried Herby Chorizo & Spinach

Ingredients

75g (3oz) chorizo sausage, chopped
2 handfuls of spinach leaves
1 handful of basil leaves, chopped
1 teaspoon olive oil

**SERVES
1**

351
calories
per serving

Method

Heat the olive oil in a frying pan, add the sausage and cook for 5 minutes, stirring occasionally. Add the spinach leaves to the frying pan and cook them for 2-3 minutes or until they've wilted. Toss in the basil leaves. Serve and eat straight away.

Mozzarella & Radicchio Salad With Pesto Dressing

Ingredients

125g (4oz) mozzarella cheese, sliced
1 large tomato, sliced
½ radicchio lettuce
1 teaspoon pesto sauce
2 teaspoons olive oil
1 tablespoon apple cider vinegar
Several basil leaves, chopped
Sea salt
Freshly ground black pepper

SERVES 1

457
calories
per serving

Method

Place the pesto sauce, olive oil, vinegar and chopped basil into a bowl and mix well.
Season with salt and pepper. Arrange the tomato slices and mozzarella slices on a plate.
Add the radicchio to the plate. Drizzle the pesto dressing over the salad. Serve and enjoy.

Chilli & Lime Cod

Ingredients

1 large cod fillet
1/2 onion, chopped
1 stalk of celery, chopped
1 clove of garlic, chopped
1 green chilli, chopped
2 tablespoons fresh coriander (cilantro), chopped
Juice of 1/2 lime
1 teaspoon olive oil
Sea salt

**SERVES
1**

248
calories
per serving

Method

Place the lime juice and a pinch of salt into a bowl and coat the fish in the mixture. Heat the olive oil in a frying pan, add in the celery, garlic and onion and cook for 3 minutes until slightly softened. Transfer the celery mixture to an ovenproof dish and add in the cod steak. Scatter the coriander (cilantro) and chilli into the dish. Transfer the dish to the oven and bake at 180C/360F and cook for around 20 minutes or until the fish is completely cooked.

Turkey & Bamboo Shoot Stir-Fry

Ingredients

50g (2oz) mushrooms, sliced
25g (1oz) bamboo shoots
25g (1oz) water chestnuts, drained
1 medium turkey steak, sliced
1/2 red pepper (bell pepper), sliced
1/4 courgette (zucchini) sliced
2 spring onions (scallions), chopped
2 teaspoons olive oil
1 teaspoon sesame oil
1 teaspoon lemon juice
1 teaspoon soy sauce
1/4 teaspoon ground ginger
1 clove of garlic, chopped

**SERVES
1**

332
calories
per serving

Method

Place the lemon juice, ginger, garlic and soy sauce in a bowl and mix well. Add in the turkey pieces and coat them well. Cover and allow to marinate for at least 30 minutes. Heat the olive oil and sesame oil in a frying pan. Add the turkey and cook for 3-4 minutes then remove it and set aside. Add the red pepper, courgette (zucchini), mushrooms, bamboo shoots and water chestnuts and cook for 3 minutes Return the turkey steaks to the frying pan and cook for another 3 minutes. Serve with cauliflower rice.

Sweet Treats & Snacks

Cheddar & Herb Crisps

Ingredients

50g (2oz) Cheddar cheese,
grated (shredded)
Sprinkling dried mixed herbs

MAKES 6 CRISPS

35 calories per crisp

Method

Place small individual piles of cheese on a baking sheet. Sprinkle the herbs on top of the cheese. Transfer the baking sheet to the oven and bake at 150C/300F for around 5 minutes or until the cheese becomes crisp. Serve on their own or with guacamole or salsa.

Carrot & Parsnip Fries

Ingredients

1 medium carrot, finely sliced
1 medium parsnip, finely sliced
2 teaspoons coconut oil, melted
1 teaspoon fresh rosemary, chopped
Sea salt
Freshly ground black pepper

**SERVES
1**

161
calories
per serving

Method

In a bowl, mix together the coconut oil, rosemary, salt and pepper. Coat the carrot and parsnip in the oil mixture. Scatter the vegetables onto a baking sheet. Transfer them to the oven and cook at 150C/300F and cook for around 25 minutes or until they are crispy. Serve on their own or with your favourite dip.

Chocolate & Coconut Cookies

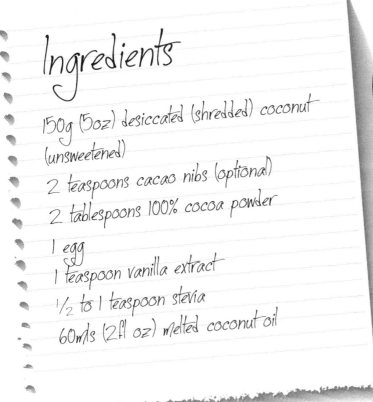

Ingredients

150g (5oz) desiccated (shredded) coconut (unsweetened)

2 teaspoons cacao nibs (optional)

2 tablespoons 100% cocoa powder

1 egg

1 teaspoon vanilla extract

½ to 1 teaspoon stevia

60mls (2fl oz) melted coconut oil

MAKES 6 COOKIES

280
calories
per cookie

Method

In a bowl, whisk the egg together with the coconut oil, stevia and vanilla extract. Sprinkle in the cocoa powder and mix well until completely combined. Stir in the desiccated (shredded) coconut and cacao nibs/chocolate chips (if using). Grease and line a baking sheet. Spoon 6 dollops of the mixture onto the baking sheet. Transfer it to the oven and bake at 190C/375F and cook for around 12 minutes. Allow to cool then store in an airtight container until ready to use.

Raspberry & Chia Seed Pudding

Ingredients

1 banana

25g (1oz) chia seeds

50g (2oz) frozen raspberries

¼ teaspoon cinnamon

120mls (4fl oz) almond milk

SERVES 1

229
calories
per serving

Method

Place the almond milk into a serving bowl, stir in the cinnamon and add the chia seeds. Cover and chill in the fridge for an hour or so. Place the banana and frozen raspberries into a blender and process until smooth. Spoon the fruit on top of the creamy chia mixture. Serve.

Cinnamon & Walnut Mug Cake

SERVES
1

447
calories
each

Ingredients

2 teaspoons ground flaxseeds (linseeds)

2 tablespoons ground almonds (almond meal/almond flour)

1 tablespoon chopped walnuts

1 egg

1/2 teaspoon vanilla extract

1/2 teaspoon baking powder

1/2 teaspoon cinnamon

1/4 teaspoon stevia (or to taste)

1 teaspoon coconut oil (melted)

Pinch of salt

Method

Mix together the egg, oil and vanilla. Add in dry ingredients and mix until completely combined. Transfer the mixture to a large microwaveable mug. Cook in the microwave on full power for around 1 ½ minutes. Allow it to cool. Enjoy.

Low Carb Chocolate Mug Cake

Ingredients

- 2 teaspoons ground flaxseeds (linseeds)
- 2 teaspoons 100% cocoa powder
- 1 egg
- 1 tablespoon coconut flour
- 1/4 teaspoon baking powder
- 1/4 teaspoon vanilla extract
- 1/2 teaspoon stevia (or to taste)
- 25mls (1 fl oz) milk
- Pinch of salt
- Oil for greasing

SERVES 1

185 calories per serving

Method

In a bowl, mix together the coconut flour, flaxseeds (linseeds), cocoa powder, stevia, baking powder and salt. In a separate bowl, mix together the egg, milk and vanilla extract. Add in the dry mixture to the egg mixture and mix well. Grease a microwaveable mug with a little vegetable oil. Spoon the mixture into the mug. Cook in the microwave on full power for around 1 ½ minutes. Let it cool slightly and enjoy.

High Protein Chocolate Peanut Butter Biscuits

Ingredients

225g (8oz) tinned chickpeas (garbanzo beans), drained
125g (4oz) peanut butter
3 tablespoons 100% cocoa powder
1 teaspoon vanilla extract
1 teaspoon stevia sweetener (optional)
1 teaspoon baking powder
200mls (7fl oz) almond milk

MAKES 12

101 calories per biscuit

Method

Place all of the ingredients into a blender and process until smooth. You can add a little extra almond milk to thin the mixture if required. Scoop out 12 small spoonfuls (or 6 for large cookies) of the mixture and place them on a baking tray. Transfer them to an oven, preheated to 200C/400F and cook for 15 minutes.

Almond & Banana Ice Cream

Ingredients

- 1 banana
- 2 teaspoons almond butter
- 75mls (3fl oz) almond milk
- ½ teaspoon vanilla essence
- Pinch of salt

SERVES 1

157
calories
per serving

Method

Place all of the ingredients into a food processor and blitz until smooth and creamy. Pour the mixture into a container and place it in the freezer (or an ice-cream maker if you have one). Whisk it with a fork after 1 hour and return it to the freezer. You can easily multiply the ingredients quantities to make a larger batch to store in the freezer.

Lime & Coconut Truffles

Ingredients

100g (3½ oz) cream cheese

25g (1oz) creamed coconut

3 tablespoons unsweetened desiccated (shredded) coconut

2 teaspoons coconut oil

1 teaspoon stevia sweetener (or to taste)

Juice of 1 lime

Pinch of salt

1 tablespoons desiccated (shredded) coconut for rolling

MAKES 6

120 calories per truffle

Method

Place coconut oil, creamed coconut and cream cheese into a blender and mix well. Add in the desiccated coconut, lime juice, salt and stevia and combine them. Chill in the fridge for 1 hour. Shape the mixture into ball shapes. Scatter the coconut for rolling on a plate and roll the truffles in them, coating them well. Store in the fridge until ready to use.

Quick Blueberry & Lemon Cheesecake Mug

Ingredients

50g (2oz) cream cheese
25g (1oz) blueberries
2 tablespoons crème fraîche
1 egg
1 teaspoon lemon juice
½ teaspoon vanilla extract
½ teaspoon stevia extract (or to taste)

SERVES 1

229
calories
per serving

Method

Place all the ingredients, except the blueberries, into a large mug or a microwaveable bowl and mix well. Cook in the microwave for 30 seconds, remove and stir then return it to the microwave for another 30 seconds, remove and stir. Return it to the microwave for another 30 seconds. Chill in the fridge before serving. Serve with a scattering of blueberries.

Creamy Apple Noodles

Ingredients

1 large apple, peeled and cored
1 tablespoon ground almonds (almond meal/almond flour)
¼ teaspoon stevia sweetener (optional)
½ teaspoon olive oil
1-2 teaspoons water (optional)
Large pinch of cinnamon
Pinch of salt
1 tablespoon crème fraîche

**SERVES
1**

171
calories
per serving

Method

Use a spiraliser to cut the apple into long noodle pieces. Don't worry if you don't have a spiraliser, just cut the apple into thin strips instead. Place the apple noodles into a bowl and sprinkle in the ground almonds (almond meal/almond flour) stevia (if using) cinnamon and salt. Heat the olive oil in a frying pan, add the apple and cook until the apple has softened. Add in the water if the apple sticks to the pan and needs moisture. Serve with a dollop of crème fraîche.

Banana Cream

Ingredients

1 frozen banana
2 teaspoons almond butter
2 tablespoons crème fraîche

**SERVES
1**

170
calories
per serving

Method

Chop the banana and place it in a bowl, add the almond butter and top if off with the crème fraîche. Eat straight away.

You may also be interested in other titles by
Erin Rose Publishing
which are available in both paperback and ebook.

 Quick Start Guides

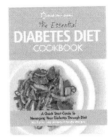

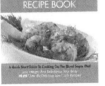

Books by Sophie Ryan
Erin Rose Publishing

30 Simple And Delicious Superfood Energy Balls And Bites
Recipes For Great Health and Wellbeing

Over 30 Easy And Delicious Superfood Energy Bars
Recipes To Boost Your Vitality

30 Simple And Tasty Energy Shots And Smoothies
To Power Up Your Health And Well-Being

Printed in Great Britain
by Amazon